MEGA ACTIVITY BOOK FOR MINECRAFT FANS

Copyright © 2017 Steve Stevenson

All rights reserved

NOT AN OFFICIAL MINECRAFT PRODUCT. NOT APPROVED BY OR ASSOCIATED WITH MOJANG.

PICTURE PUZZLES

1. WHICH OCELOT?

Only one of the small Minecraft ocelot pictures is exactly the same as the big one. Can you see which one it is?

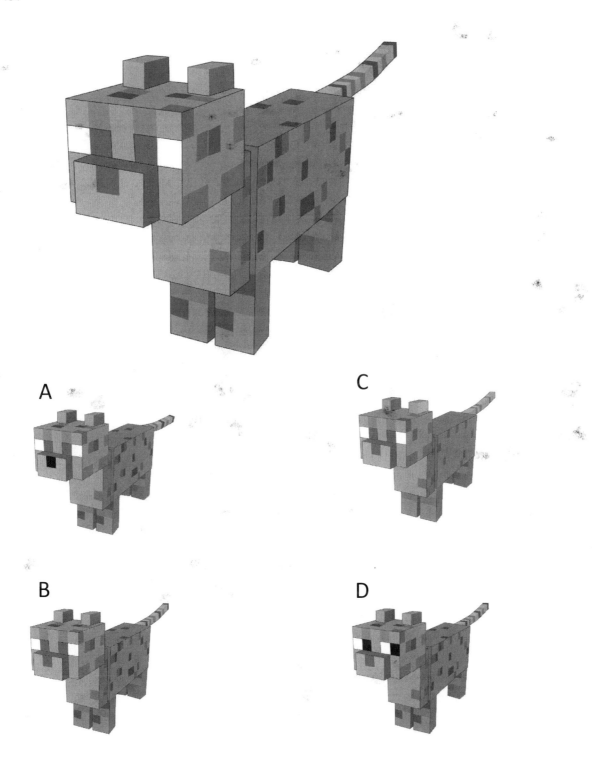

PICTURE PUZZLES
2. DOT TO DOT

Join all the numbered dots in number order to complete the picture of a Minecraft mob.

PICTURE PUZZLES
3. WHICH CREEPER?

Only one of the little creepers is exactly the same as the one in the bigger picture. Can you spot which one?

A

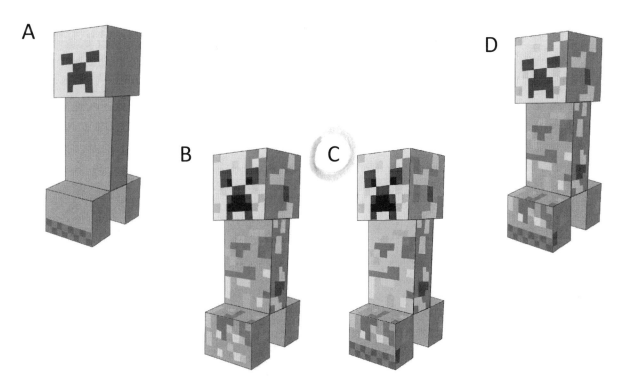

B

C

D

PICTURE PUZZLES
4. SPOT THE DIFFERENCE

There are six differences between the two pictures. Can you spot all of them?

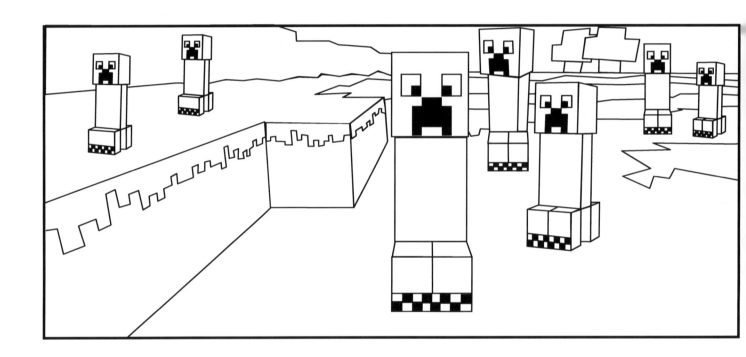

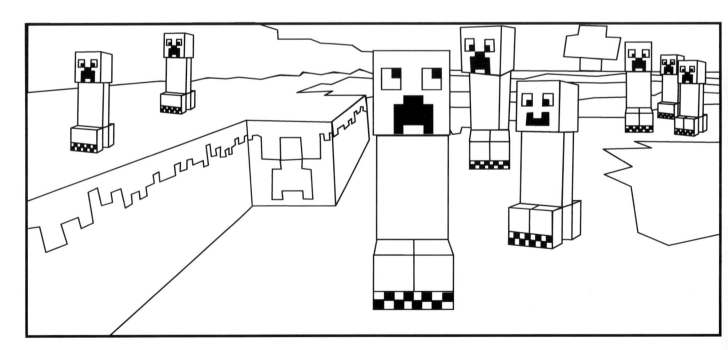

PICTURE PUZZLES
5. DOT TO DOT

Join all the numbered dots in number order to complete the mob picture.

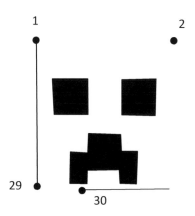

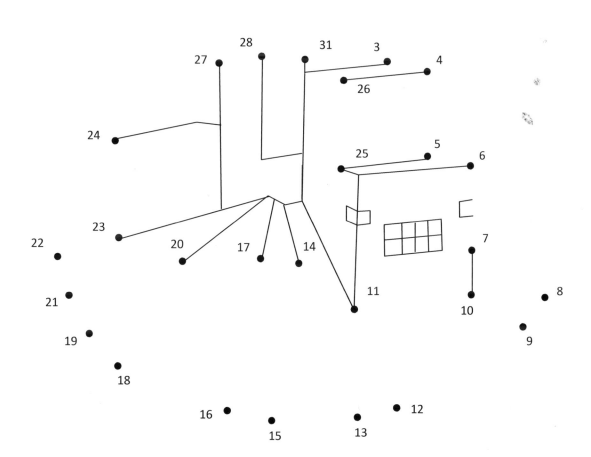

PICTURE PUZZLES
6. WHICH PIG?

Only one of the smaller pigs is exactly the same as the big Minecraft pig picture. Spot which one it is.

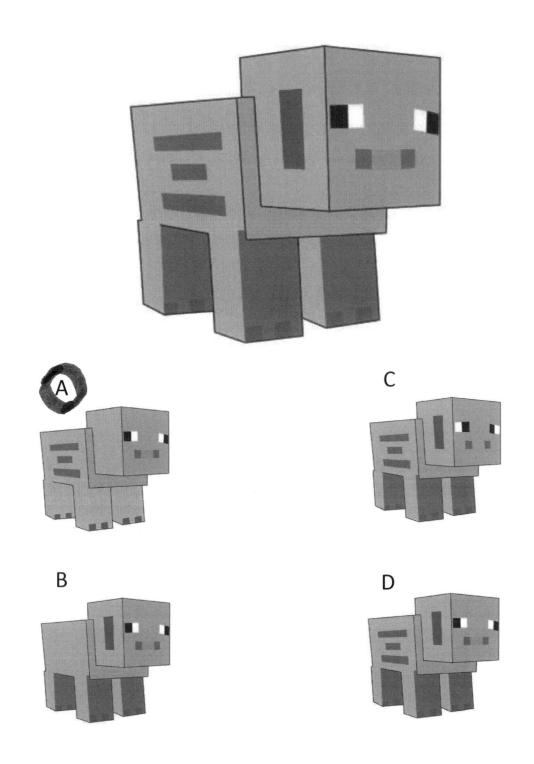

PICTURE PUZZLES
7. DOT TO DOT

Join all the numbered dots from 1 to 20 to complete the Minecraft mob picture.

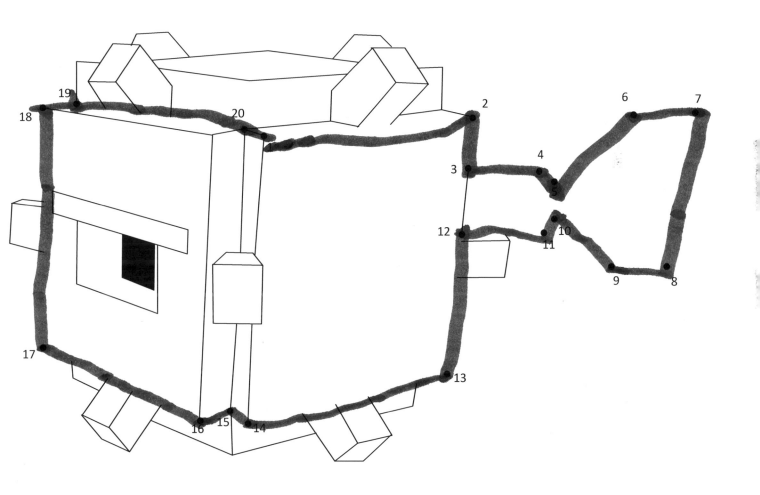

PICTURE PUZZLES
8. WHICH RABBIT?

Only one Minecraft rabbit is exactly the same as the big picture. Spot which one it is.

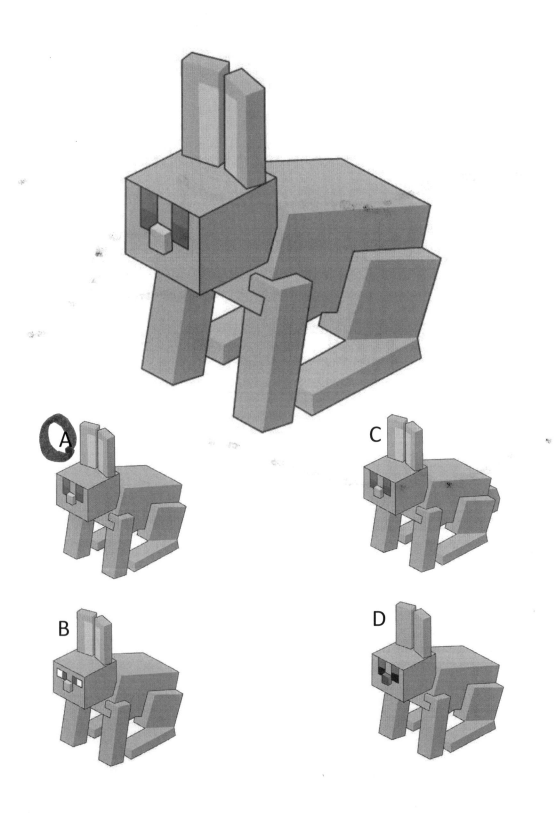

PICTURE PUZZLES
9. DOT TO DOT

Join all the numbered dots in number order from 1 to 50 to complete the picture of a Minecraft tool.

PICTURE PUZZLES
10. WHICH WOLF?

Only one of these Minecraft wolves is exactly the same as the one in the bigger picture. Can you work out which?

PICTURE PUZZLES

11. SPOT THE DIFFERENCE

There are six differences between the two pictures. Can you spot all of them?

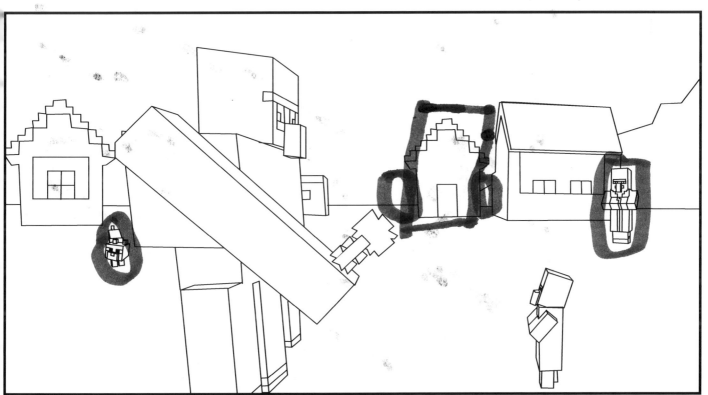

PICTURE PUZZLES
12. DOT TO DOT

Very carefully, join all the numbered dots in number order to complete the picture of a tameable mob.

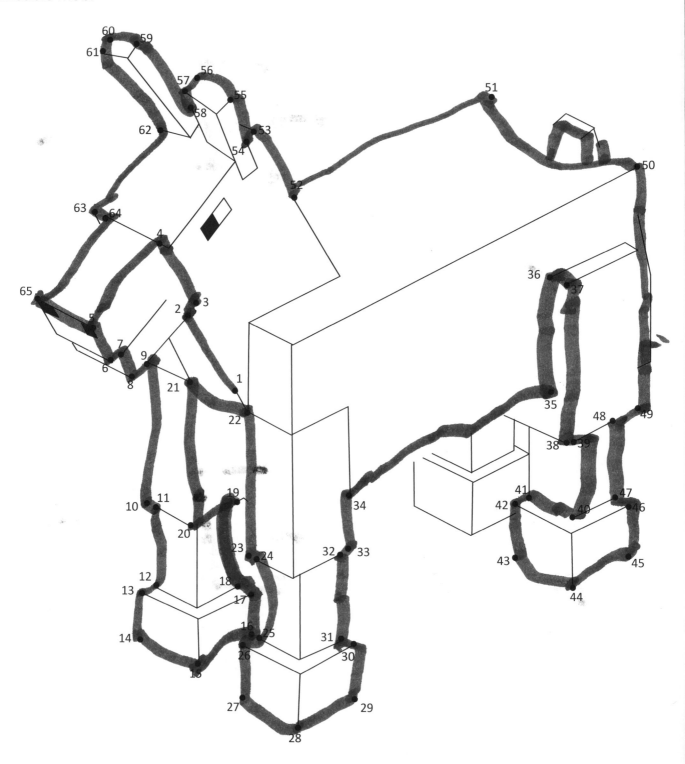

PICTURE PUZZLES
13. WHICH SKELETON?

Only one of the small skeleton pictures is exactly the same as the big one. Can you see which one it is?

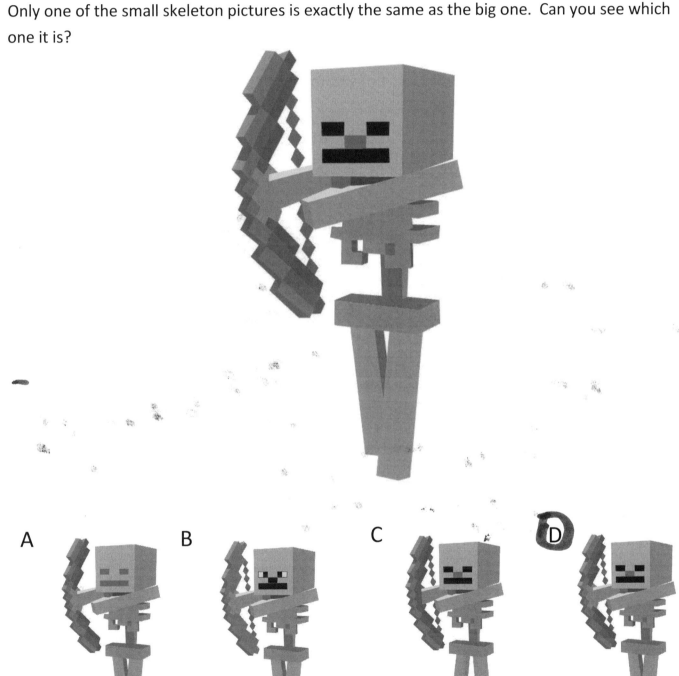

A   B   C   D

PICTURE PUZZLES
14. DOT TO DOT

Join all the numbered dots in number order to complete the mob picture.

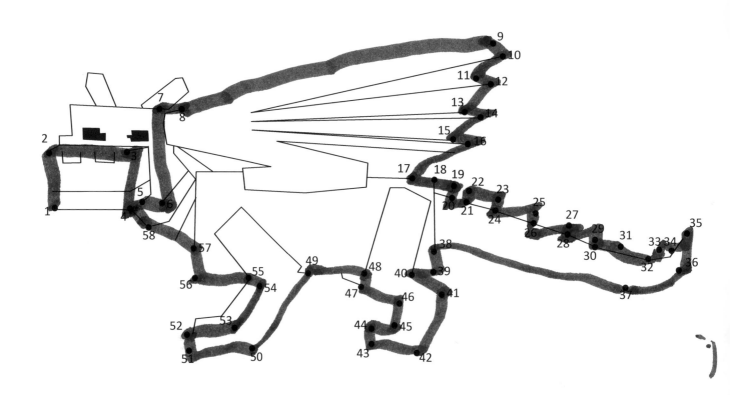

PICTURE PUZZLES
15. WHICH ENDERMAN

Only one of the small Enderman pictures is exactly the same as the big one. Can you spot which?

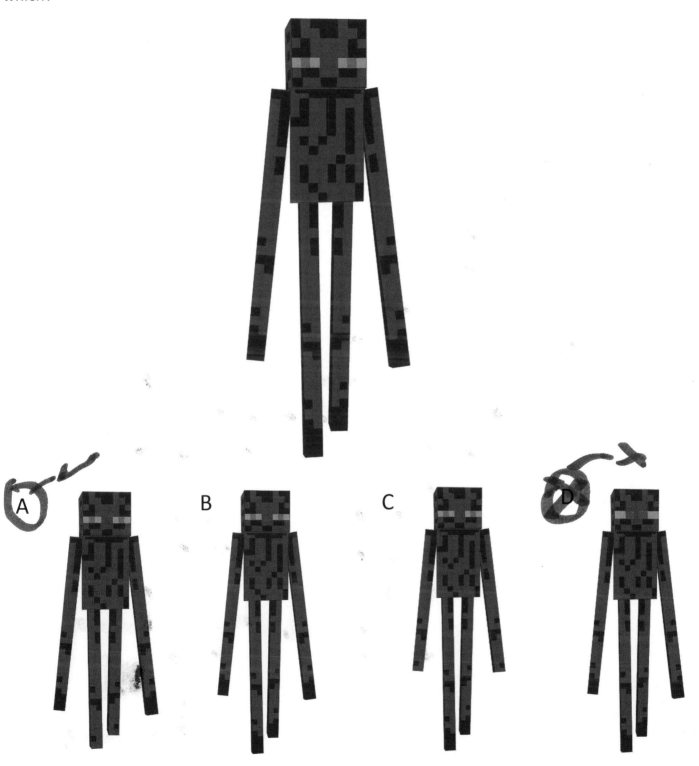

A   B   C   D

PICTURE PUZZLES
16. DOT TO DOT

Join all the numbered dots in number order to make a picture of a Minecraft item.

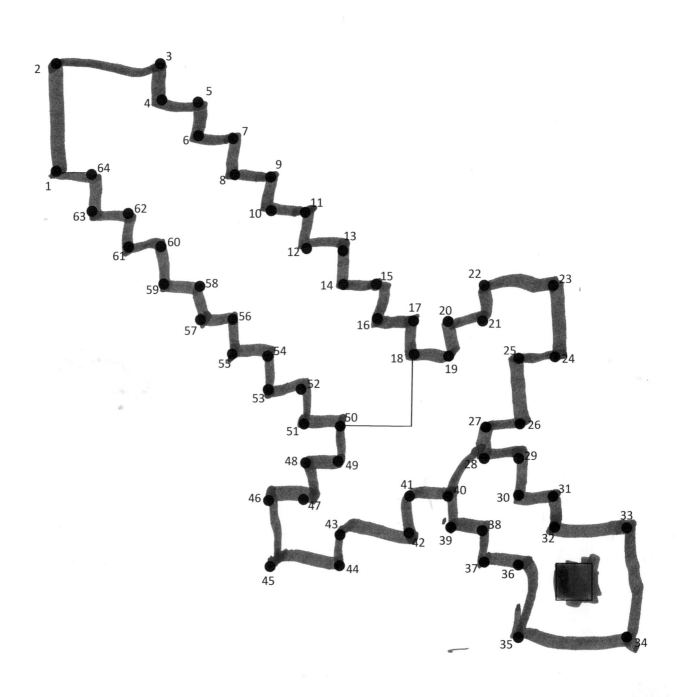

WORDSEARCH
17. BOSS MOBS WORDSEARCH

Words are hidden in the grid forwards, backwards, up, down, or diagonally. Ignore any spaces or punctuation - for instance, if "DRAGON'S BREATH" is listed, look for "DRAGONSBREATH".

```
B R E S D E R T D N E E H T S
L R G S W D S L K L N A E R A
L M G Y S I H J N O D S D E R
U D R A G O N S B R E A T H E
K G E K T N B J K Y R U K E M
S A S A Y O I U Y G C U H N N
R R A D D T H H B T H H U E I
E Q W T N L G S C E A G S H U
H T R R S D Y B L B R D R T H
T L E T U E L U A V G O E I T
I E R L R E H T I W E H T K R
W M V D N A S L U O S B T L F
T N B N O G A R D R E D N E C
```

ENDER DRAGON
THE WITHER
THE NETHER
THE END
DEADLY
BOSS
ENDER CHARGES
DRAGON'S BREATH
SOUL SAND
WITHER SKULL

18. CREEPER WORDSEARCH

```
A D R E T H E R G Y U I O P L
S B V T D E G R A H C R Y B B
H I S S S C V N Y T H U O R O
I K I U J H W B V G E M H K O
D W R K E A R J G R Y J E K M
E D F E P B Y U Y E S Q L X C
E S E S P E R G J E I O I M K
D D R B R E T G Y N I E T P K
H T O B R D E E W D R E S R H
G L S L R F L R U G J H O I O
M N O I P N H U C T D S H W L
W E R D S X E R T Y V B F U I
T R E W A Q E D R R E G N A D
```

CREEPER
GREEN
HISS
EXPLODE
DANGER
HOSTILE
BOOM
MOB
CHARGED
SPAWN

WORDSEARCH
19. PIG WORDSEARCH

```
P G E H I U E D I U T S G E D
R E G G H R L F U I B I E P R
F P O R K C H O P O R S R O T
K H E E E N I T B P E I P L W
A I S A D D L E H L E S I R D
E P L N T M R B I E D I G E R
U O O H R F P N U R S S L D U
Q L S R E T T O R T E I E S G
S S I K S I S G R S R S T R R
V E U L D E L K N I O E E T T
B T T G E R D U W A W S D E D
N R I O R S N O U T D I R I I
M P G E F B F W E E R S N A R
```

PIG
OINK
SQUEAK
SADDLE
RIDE
PORKCHOP
PIGLET
BREED
SNOUT
TROTTERS

20. SKELETON WORDSEARCH

```
P G E H I U E D I U T S G E D
R E S E N O B F S I G I E A R
F R R T B H O E N K T S R R T
T H O R S E M A N P U I H R W
B I D R R H U R Y L E L I O D
E O L N T M R B I A D I L W R
S O W H R F P N U R R S O S U
S K E L E T O N G W E T L S G
W S E L I T S O H S R S S R R
V E U L D E L Y T D T I E T T
B N O T E L E K S R E H T I W
N R H U N D E A D V D I R R R
M N G E F B F W E E R S N A E
```

SKELETON
BOW
ARROWS
UNDEAD
BONES
HOSTILE
SKULL
WITHER SKELETON
STRAY
HORSEMAN

WORDSEARCH
21. TAMEABLE MOBS WORDSEARCH

```
P G E H I U E D I U T S G E D
R E G H S I F G L I G W E P R
F R R T B H O E N O T S O O T
T S A D D L E T B P T I H L W
R I D R R H U R H E E S I R F
E P L N T M R B I L D H P E R
S E N O B F P M U B S O O D U
Y L P U E U U R G A E R L T G
E S I K S L S G R E R S S O R
K E U L E D L Y T M T E E L T
N T M I E R D U W A W S T E W
O R V O U T L H R T D I R C R
D N G E B S F W E E R S N O E
```

TAMEABLE
MOB
WOLF
BONES
OCELOT
FISH
MULE
DONKEY
HORSE
SADDLE

22. BIOMES WORDSEARCH

```
P G E D E S E R T U T S G I D
A E G G H R L F U I G T E C R
N R R T B H O E N S T A R E T
N J U N G L E T B W T I H P W
A I D R R H U R H A E G I L D
V P L E M O I B I M D A P A R
A O O H R F P N U P S S O I U
S L M U S L L I H L E I L N G
W S I E S I S G R A R S S S R
V E U L S E L Y T N T I E T T
B T T I E A D U W D W S T E W
N R H O N A E C O P E E D R R
M N G E F B F W E E R S N A E
```

BIOME
TAIGA
SWAMPLAND
HILLS
MESA
SAVANNA
DESERT
DEEP OCEAN
ICE PLAINS
JUNGLE

WORDSEARCH
23. NEUTRAL MOBS WORDSEARCH

Find all the words in the grid. Remember to ignore any spaces.

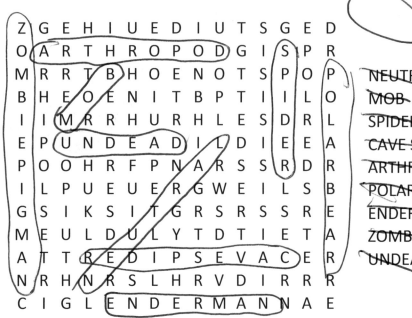

```
Z G E H I U E D I U T S G E D
O A R T H R O P O D G I S P R
M R R T B H O E N O T S P O P
B H E O E N I T B P T I L R O
I I M R R H U R H L E S D R L
E P U N D E A D I L D I E E A
P O O H R F P N A R S S R D R
I L P U E U E R G W E I L S B
G S I K S I T G R S R S S R E
M E U L D U L Y T D T I E T A
A T T R E D I P S E V A C E R
N R H N R S L H R V D I R R R
C I G L E N D E R M A N N A E
```

NEUTRAL
MOB
SPIDER
CAVE SPIDER
ARTHROPOD
POLAR BEAR
ENDERMAN
ZOMBIE PIGMAN
UNDEAD

24. RABBIT WORDSEARCH

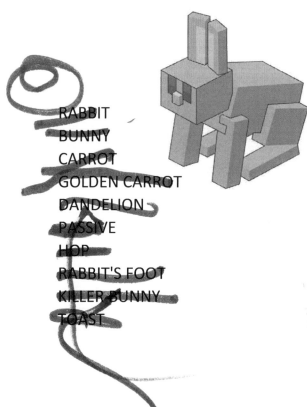

```
M N R E F B F W E B U N N Y E
P D A N D E L I O N T C G E D
R E B G H R L F U I G A E K R
E R B E U P L P O H T R R I T
D R I O V E S A B P T R H L W
R I T R R I U R H L E O I L D
E P S N T M S B I E D T P E R
S O F H R F P S U R L J O R U
A G O L D E N C A R R O T B G
W S O K S I S G R P R S S U R
V E T L D E L Y T D T I E N T
B T T I E T O A S T W S T N W
N R H O R S T I B B A R L Y R
```

RABBIT
BUNNY
CARROT
GOLDEN CARROT
DANDELION
PASSIVE
HOP
RABBIT'S FOOT
KILLER BUNNY
TOAST

WORDSEARCH
25. OCELOT WORDSEARCH

```
R O E B U I E R I U T S G E D
O U C G H R L A U R G I F P R
D S T E U P L W N A T S U O T
V I U O L E S F B W T H R L W
R A D R R O U L H S E S I R D
E M L N T M T S T A I L P Y R
S E O H R F P H U L S F O B U
A S P U E U E M G M E W L B G
W E I T S I S G R O R A S A Y
V O A H D E L Y T N T R E T O
B C T I E R D U W A W S T E W
N R P U R R L H G N I T T I S
M N G E F B F W E E R S N A E
```

OCELOT
CAT
RAW FISH
RAW SALMON
SITTING
FUR
TAIL
PURR
TABBY
SIAMESE

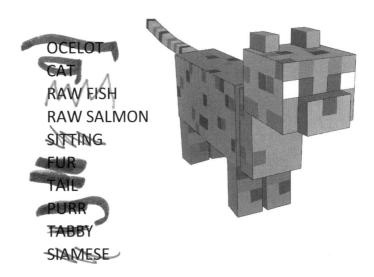

26. THE NETHER WORDSEARCH

```
A D F Y T U E D I U T S G E D
N E T H E R F O R T R E S S N
B R T B U P L E N O T S R O A
A R U O E B U C A M G A M L M
S I D R R H U R H L E S I R G
W I T H E R S K E L E T O N I
B T S A H G P N U R S S O D P
K L P U E U E M G W A I L S E
I N E T H E R R A C K V S R I
U E U L D E L Y T D T I A T B
T H E N E T H E R R A W S T L M
T R H O E N O T S W O L G R O
F E Z A L B F W E E R S N A Z
```

THE NETHER
LAVA
NETHER FORTRESS
NETHERRACK
GLOWSTONE
WITHER SKELETON
BLAZE
GHAST
ZOMBIE PIGMAN
MAGMA CUBE

WORDSEARCH

27. ENCHANTMENTS WORDSEARCH

```
P G E H I U E D I S T A G E D
U F O R T U N E U M G F E P R
E R T B U P L E N I T B R O T
D R U O P E S A B T T Y H L W
G N I L L H A F R E H T A E F
E P L N T S S E N P R A H S G
S N O I T A R I P S E R O D N
A L P U E U E M G S E M L S I
W H C U O T K L I S N R S R T
V E U L D E L Y T D T R E T O
F I R E P R O T E C T I O N O
N R H O R S L H R V D N R H L
M F I R E A S P E C T C N A T
```

FIRE PROTECTION
FEATHER FALLING
THORNS
RESPIRATION
SMITE
SHARPNESS
LOOTING
FIRE ASPECT
SILK TOUCH
FORTUNE

28. ILLAGERS WORDSEARCH

```
I B E M E R A L D S T S G T O
T V G G H H L F U I G I R P L
L I T B U O L E N O R S E O M
D N U O P S S A B O T I G L R
R D D R R T U R N L E S A R E
E I L N T I R A I E D I L E K
S C O H R L X N U R S S L X O
A A P U E E E E G W E V I S V
W T I K S M S G V S R S S R E
T O T E M O F U N D Y I N G C
P R T I E B D U W A W S T E E
N O I S N A M D N A L D O O W
C N G E F B F W E X R S N A S
```

ILLAGER
VINDICATOR
EVOKER
WOODLAND MANSION
IRON AXE
VEX
HOSTILE MOB
TOTEM OF UNDYING
EMERALDS

WORDSEARCH

29. JUNGLE TREK WORDSEARCH

```
L G E H I U E D I U T S G E D
O U I P J R L F U S G I E P R
F R S B U P L E N O T S R S T
L R T O N E S R B P T I H D W
O I O R G H E R H L E S I O D
W P L N L F M B I E D I P P R
E O E E E R T E L G N U J A U
R L C U B U E M L W E I L O G
S S O K I I S G R O R S S C R
V E U L O E L Y T D N I E O T
B T T I M R D U W A W S T C W
E L P M E T E L G N U J R R R
M N G E F S E N I V R S N A E
```

JUNGLE BIOME
JUNGLE TREE
JUNGLE TEMPLE
COCOA PODS
MELONS
FERNS
FLOWERS
VINES
OCELOTS

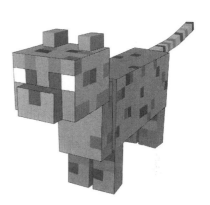

30. GOLEMS WORDSEARCH

```
P O W E R F U L S U T S G E D
O U G G H R L E U I G I I P R
P T T B U U I E N O T I R O T
R I U O Y P S A B P T R O L W
O L D R P M E L O G W O N S D
T I L O T M R B I E D N I N R
E T P H R F P N U R S G N O U
C Y H G N I K L U H E O G W G
T M I L N E L Y T D R L O B R
I O U I E O D U W A T E T A T
O B T O R S R H R V W M S L W
N R H E F B F T E E D I R L R
M N O D A I N M S E R S N S E
```

IRON GOLEM
SNOW GOLEM
UTILITY MOB
HULKING
STRONG
POWERFUL
PROTECTION
IRON INGOTS
POPPIES
SNOWBALLS

WORDSEARCH

31. THE END WORDSEARCH

```
D G E D I U E D I E T S G T O
T E I N H R L F U N G I E P E
L O T B U P L E N D T S E O X
V R U O P E S A B E T I N L I
R I T H E E N D H R E S D R T
E P L N T M R B I M D I S E P
S O E N D P O R T A L S T D O
A L P U E U E M G N E I O S R
W S I N O G A R D R E D N E T
V E U L D E L Y T D I E T A
P E N D E R C R Y S T A L E L
O R H O R S L H R V D I R R R
C N G E F G G E N O G A R D S
```

THE END
END PORTAL
ENDERMAN
ENDER DRAGON
END STONE
VOID
ENDER CRYSTAL
EXIT PORTAL
DRAGON EGG

32. TOOLS WORDSEARCH

```
D G E H I U E D I U T S G T O
S E G F I S H I N G R O D P L
H R T B U S L E N O T S U O M
O R U O P E H A B P T I R L W
V I D R R H U E H L E S A R D
E P L N T M R B A E D I B E R
L C R A F T I N G R E C I P E
A L P U X U E M G W S I L S G
W S I K S E S G R S R S I R R
H E U L E X A K C I P I T T T
P O T I E R D U W A W S Y E E
O L E E T S D N A T N I L F R
C N G E F B F W E E R S N A S
```

PICKAXE
SHOVEL
HOE
SHEARS
FISHING ROD
AXE
FLINT AND STEEL
CRAFTING RECIPE
DURABILITY

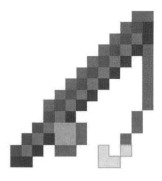

CROSSWORDS

33. CROSSWORD 1

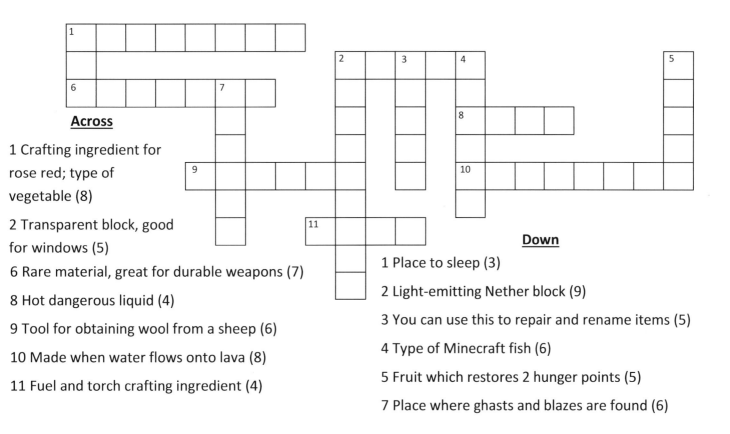

Across

1 Crafting ingredient for rose red; type of vegetable (8)

2 Transparent block, good for windows (5)

6 Rare material, great for durable weapons (7)

8 Hot dangerous liquid (4)

9 Tool for obtaining wool from a sheep (6)

10 Made when water flows onto lava (8)

11 Fuel and torch crafting ingredient (4)

Down

1 Place to sleep (3)

2 Light-emitting Nether block (9)

3 You can use this to repair and rename items (5)

4 Type of Minecraft fish (6)

5 Fruit which restores 2 hunger points (5)

7 Place where ghasts and blazes are found (6)

34. CROSSWORD 2

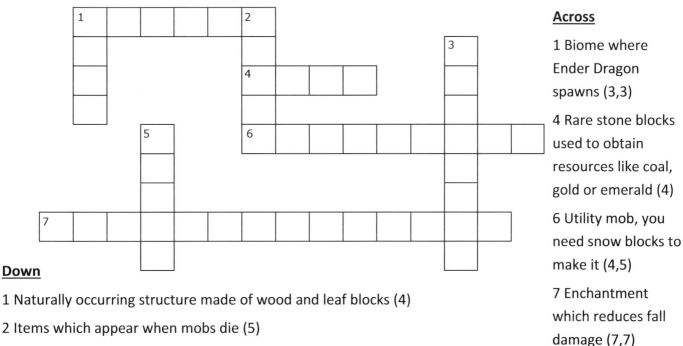

Across

1 Biome where Ender Dragon spawns (3,3)

4 Rare stone blocks used to obtain resources like coal, gold or emerald (4)

6 Utility mob, you need snow blocks to make it (4,5)

7 Enchantment which reduces fall damage (7,7)

Down

1 Naturally occurring structure made of wood and leaf blocks (4)

2 Items which appear when mobs die (5)

3 A kind of crafting using furnace blocks (8)

5 Enchantment increasing damage to undead mobs (5)

CROSSWORDS
35. CROWSSWORD 3

Across

1 You use this to brew potions (7, 5)

3 Tall black teleporting End mob (8)

6 Explosive block (initials) (3)

7 Mob which can be tamed with bones (4)

8 Block you can use to switch redstone power on and off (5)

11 Bow enchantment giving you better knockback (5)

14 Block used in redstone circuits, can be used to reduce signal strength (8,10)

15 You get this from sheep and you can dye it (4)

Down

1 Block that projects a light beam towards the sky (6)

2 Frozen water (3)

4 Special kind of paths for minecarts to travel on (5)

5 Gateway between the Overworld and the Nether (6,6)

9 This is used to store items (5)

10 You shoot this from a bow (5)

12 Biome where you find lots of trees (6)

13 Villagers are afraid of this undead mob (6)

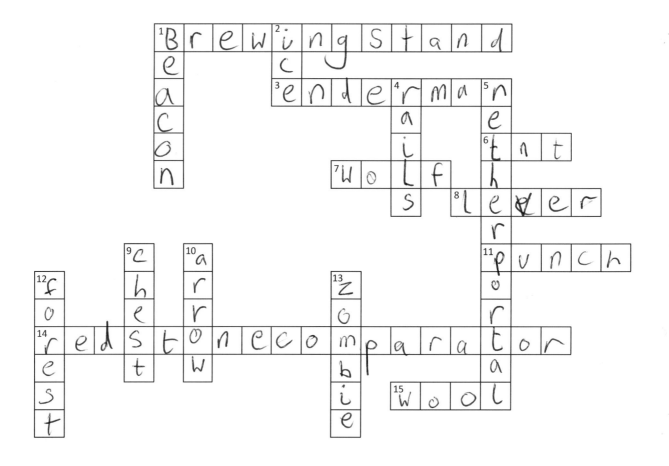

CROSSWORDS
36. CROSSWORD 4

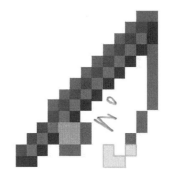

Across

1 Fishing rod enchantment (4, 2, 3, 3)

6 Armor enchantment which reduces most types of damage (10)

8 Minecraft animal found in icy places (5, 4)

11 Gemstone which is good for trades (7)

12 Fishing rod enchantment (4)

13 Pinky purplish Nether block (10)

Down

1 Sword enchantment which can make mobs drop more stuff when defeated (7)

2 Green explosive mob (7)

3 Tool for collecting wood (3)

4 Flying passive mob (3)

5 Boots enchantment which freezes water (5, 6)

7 Bow enchantment which makes arrows fiery (5)

9 Sandy biome (5)

10 Nether mob which can drop rods (5)

CROSSWORDS

37. CROSSWORD 5

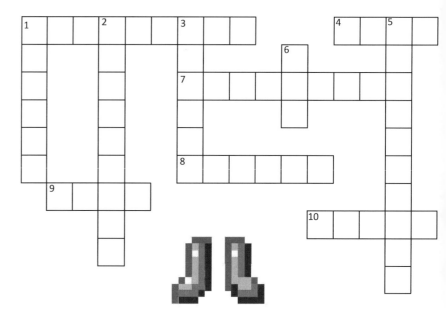

Across

1 Cow-like mob (9)

4 Zombie variant which does not burn in sunlight (4)

7 You need one of these to travel to The End (3, 6)

8 Armor enchantment which deals damage to attackers (6)

9 A kind of female version of Steve (4)

10 Underwater mob with tentacles (5)

Down

1 Creators of Minecraft (6)

2 Sword enchantment which increases damage (9)

3 Tameable mob which likes fish (6)

5 Annoying little hostile mob (10)

6 Weapon for firing arrows (3)

38. CROSSWORD 6

Across

1 Enchantment dealing increased damage to some mobs, including spiders (4, 2, 10)

4 Enchantment for increasing mining speed (10)

6 Brownish block which can be polished (7)

7 Gray block which can be polished (8)

Down

1 What you get if you give two adult pigs a carrot (4, 3)

2 Villager who catches fish (9)

3 Enchantment which pushes opponents backwards (9)

5 Passive mob that drops feathers (7)

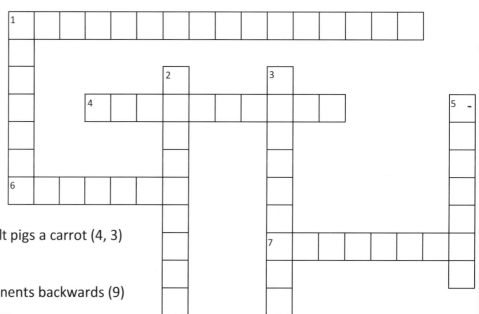

CROSSWORDS
39. CROSSWORD 7

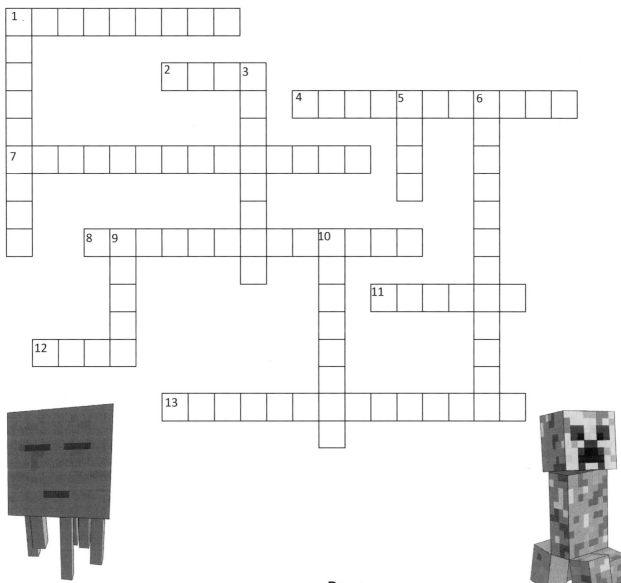

Across

1 Potion ingredient dropped by ghasts (5, 4)

2 Noise made by creepers (4)

4 Blue block (5, 6)

7 Type of skeleton that spawns in a Nether fortress (6, 8)

8 Baby zombie riding a chicken (7, 6)

11 Carrot-loving passive mob which comes in a variant called Toast (6)

12 Tameable mob bred from a horse and a donkey (4)

13 Rare biome with mycelium instead of grass on the surface (8, 6)

Down

1 Explosive substance (9)

3 Nether block which slows down players and mobs (4,4)

5 Common block found in beaches and deserts, crafting ingredient for TNT (4)

6 Pink and green undead Nether mob (6, 6)

9 Rideable tameable mob, which can also come in a zombie or skeleton variety (5)

10 Item which can hold water, and in pocket edition, can also hold potions and dyed water (8)

CROSSWORDS
40. CROSSWORD 8

Across

2 Crafting ingredient for an arrow dropped by a chicken (7)

4 Neutral mob which can inflict poisoning (4, 6)

7 Tameable mob which can be bred with hay bales (5)

8 Block which can transmit redstone power (8, 4)

Down

1 Flying hostile mob, spawns as part of an evoker's summoning attack (3)

2 Sword enchantment which sets the opponent on fire (4, 6)

3 Helmet enchantment, increases underwater breathing time (11)

4 Item for telling the time (5)

5 Place where villagers live (7)

6 Purple hostile mob found in End Cities (7)

41. CROSSWORD 9

Across

1 Armor enchantment which reduces explosion damage (5, 10)

5 Food item which can be cooked and eaten baked (6)

6 Water-filled biome (5)

7 Tool for lighting a fire (5, 3, 5)

Down

1 Skeleton drop used to tame a wolf (4)

2 Passive mob which drops wool (5)

3 Food item which is an ingredient for a type of pie (7)

4 Something which TNT and creepers do (7)

CROSSWORDS
42. CROSSWORD 10

Across

1 Place where illagers spawn (8, 7)

4 Throwable potion (6, 6)

7 Skeleton which shoots arrows that inflict slowness (5)

8 Damage taken as a result of dropping from a height (4, 6)

9 Block for pushing, can be sticky or regular (6)

10 Potion increasing jump height and reducing fall damage (7)

11 Minecraft's smallest hostile mob (9)

Down

1 Food item needed to craft bread, cake and cookies (5)

2 Items used to change colors, for example the color of wool or leather (4)

3 Bluey-greeny-greyish block from ocean monuments (10)

5 Type of potion which causes 6 damage (7)

6 Dark time of day when hostile mobs spawn in the Overworld (9)

CROSSWORDS
43. CROSSWORD 11

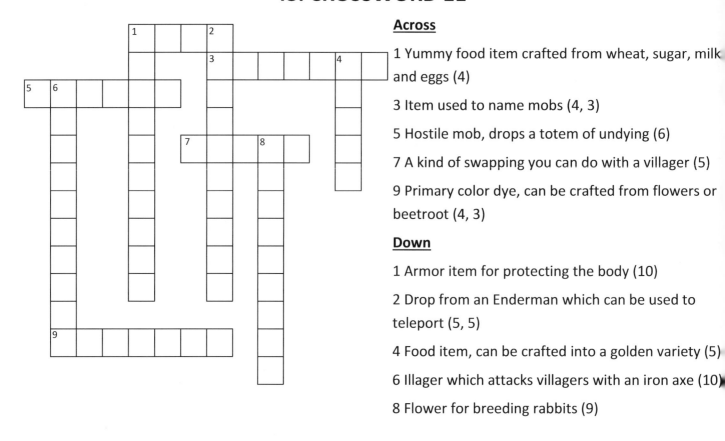

Across

1 Yummy food item crafted from wheat, sugar, milk and eggs (4)

3 Item used to name mobs (4, 3)

5 Hostile mob, drops a totem of undying (6)

7 A kind of swapping you can do with a villager (5)

9 Primary color dye, can be crafted from flowers or beetroot (4, 3)

Down

1 Armor item for protecting the body (10)

2 Drop from an Enderman which can be used to teleport (5, 5)

4 Food item, can be crafted into a golden variety (5)

6 Illager which attacks villagers with an iron axe (10)

8 Flower for breeding rabbits (9)

44. CROSSWORD 12

Across

1 Dark red and black slime-like Nether mob (5, 4)

4 Utility mob which protects villagers (4, 5)

7 Villager who wears a green robe (6)

8 Item which appears when mobs die (4)

Down

1 Food obtained by milking a mooshroom (8,4)

2 Food item which can be thrown to knock back an enemy (3)

3 Food items which can be used to dye things brown (5, 5)

5 Liquid crafting ingredient for cake (4)

6 Melee weapon with blade (5)

KRISS KROSS

45. KRISS KROSS 1

All of the words in the lists can be fitted into the grid. Work out where they go.

4 letters	5 letters	6 letters	8 letters	9 letters
LAVA	CHEST	BEACON	BEETROOT	SANDSTONE
SLAB	GLASS	COBWEB	ENDERMAN	
	LEVER	GRAVEL	OBSIDIAN	
	MELON	LADDER	REDSTONE	
	STONE	PODZOL	TRIPWIRE	
	TORCH	PORTAL		
	WATER	SPONGE		

KRISS KROSS

46. KRISS KROSS 2

Fit all the words into the grid. There is only one way they will all fit properly.

4 letters	5 letters	6 letters	7 letters	8 letters	10 letters
DOOR	GLASS	BUTTON	BEDROCK	DETECTOR	NETHERRACK
DUST	SLABS	FLOWER	DROPPER	TRAPDOOR	SEALANTERN
IRON		HOPPER	JUKEBOX		
RAIL		LEAVES	PISTONS		
SNOW		PORTAL	SAPLING		
WOOL		POTATO			

KRISS KROSS

47. KRISS KROSS 3

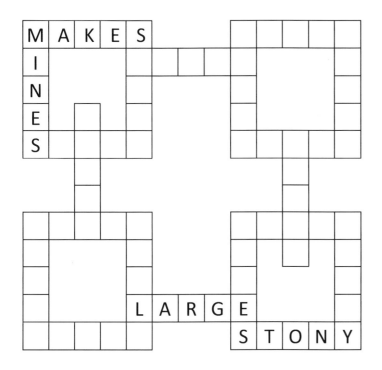

Fit all these five letter words into the grid. Some words have been put in already to help you get started.

ENEMY	SHEEP
FIGHT	RAIDS
FLESH	SLIME
HILLS	SLIMY
MAKES	STEVE
MELEE	STONE
MODES	TORCH
PARRY	TRAPS

48. KRISS KROSS 4

Work out how these words fit into the grid. Some words have been written in already, to help you get started.

6 letters
DONKEY
RAINED
SHOVEL
STEAKS
VALLEY

7 letters
VILLAGE
GRANITE
PICKAXE

8 letters
EMERALDS
GRIEFERS
REDSTONE
SPEAKING
VILLAGER

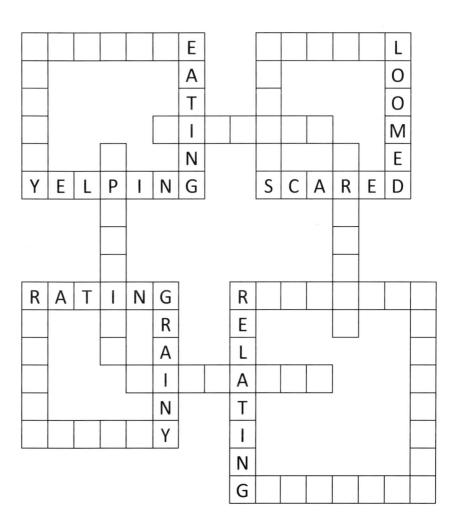

KRISS KROSS
49. KRISS KROSS 5

Fit all the words from the lists into the grid.   All of them are 7 letters long. Some words have been put in for you already, to help you get started.

ARSENAL   PICKAXE
DEMANDS   POTIONS
DURABLE   REGAINS
ENEMIES   SADDLES
EXPLODE   SHULKER
GLARING   SMELTED
GLISTEN   WEATHER

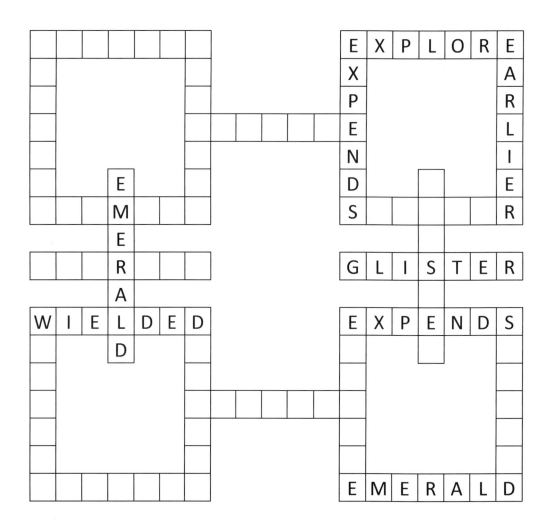

KRISS KROSS

50. KRISS KROSS 6

3 letters
BED
BOW
HOE
ORE
ROD

4 letters
CAKE
TAME
TRAP
WOLF

6 letters
BIOMES
CLOCKS
CRAFTS
FLOWER
FOREST
SADDLE
SWORDS
WITHER

8 letters
OBSIDIAN
PICKAXES
SHULKERS

9 letters
DANDELION
SWAMPLAND

KRISS KROSS
51. KRISS KROSS 7

3 letters
BAT
BED
COW
ICE
TNT
VEX

4 letters
ALEX

5 letters
ANVIL
BEACH
DROPS
FLAME
PUNCH
RAILS
SMITE

6 letters
CLERIC
NETHER
SHEARS

7 letters
ILLAGER
BREWING

9 letters
ARTHROPOD
BABY SHEEP
FISHERMAN
GLOWSTONE

10 letters
EFFICIENCY
PROTECTION
PUFFERFISH

11 letters
FROST WALKER

KRISS KROSS

52. KRISS KROSS 8

4 letters
HUSK
RAIL
TREE
WOOL

5 letters
BLAZE
SQUID

6 letters
MOJANG
OCELOT
SALMON
THE END
THORNS
ZOMBIE

7 letters
DIAMOND

9 letters
END PORTAL
KNOCKBACK
MOOSHROOM
SNOW GOLEM

KRISS KROSS
53. KRISS KROSS 9

3 letters
PIE
ROD
TNT

4 letters
CAKE
LAKE
STEW
TREE

5 letters
BREAD
LLAMA
SUGAR
WIELD

6 letters
COOKIE

7 letters
ATTACKS
CREEPER

8 letters
ANDESITE
MUSHROOM
SMELTING

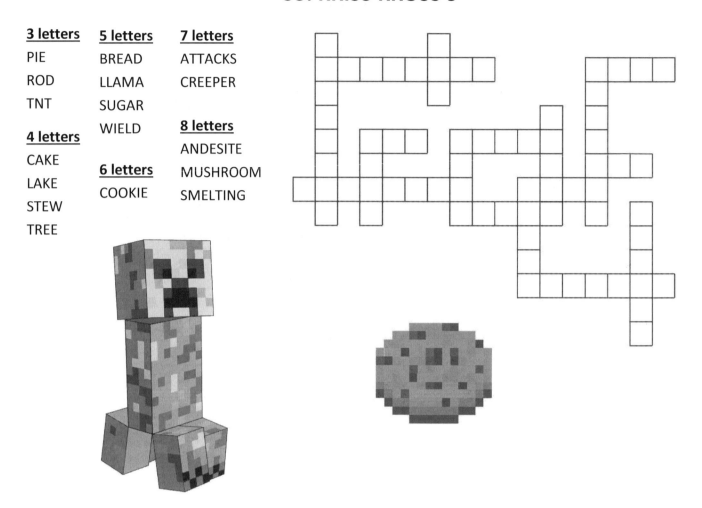

54. KRISS KROSS 10

4 letters
DROP
HITS
LUCK
MAKE
MEND
TOOL
USES

6 letters
GOLEMS
STAMPY

7 letters
GLACIER

10 letters
PUMPKIN PIE
SILVERFISH

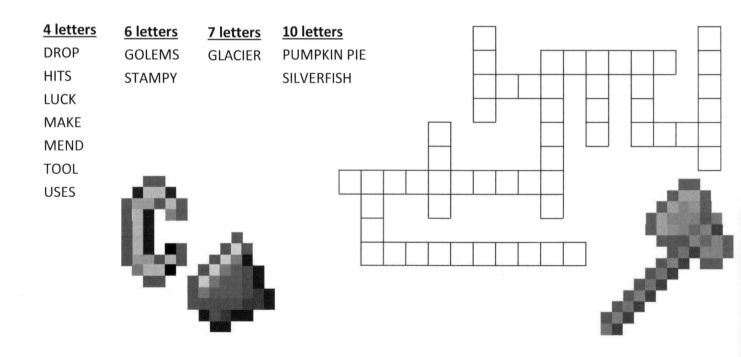

KRISS KROSS
55. KRISS KROSS 11

4 letters
VOID
ORES

6 letters
COBWEB
EVOKER
SPONGE

7 letters
CARROTS
MISSILE

10 letters
BABY HORSES
BABY WOLVES
PRISMARINE
VINDICATOR

9 letters
SHARPNESS

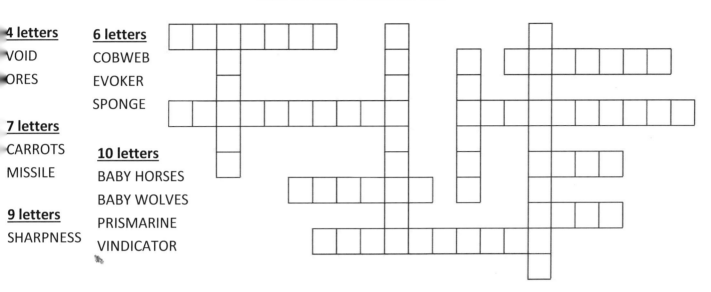

56. KRISS KROSS 12

3 letters
END
MOB
MOD
WEB

4 letters
BANE
BEAN
BONE

5 letters
BLOCK
DOORS
INGOT
KILLS
LAKES
SLIME
VINES

6 letters
BRICKS
DAMAGE
STONES
WOLVES

MAZES

57. HUNGRY LIKE THE WOLF

Show Wolfy the Minecraft wolf the path through the maze to find the bone.

MAZES

58. WEB QUEST

This character has a new sword with the Bane of Arthropods enchantment. Show him the path to the centre of the web so he can try it out by battling the spider.

MAZES

59. SHOW DOLLY THE WAY

Show Dolly the Minecraft sheep the way to the middle of the maze so she can reach the wheat.

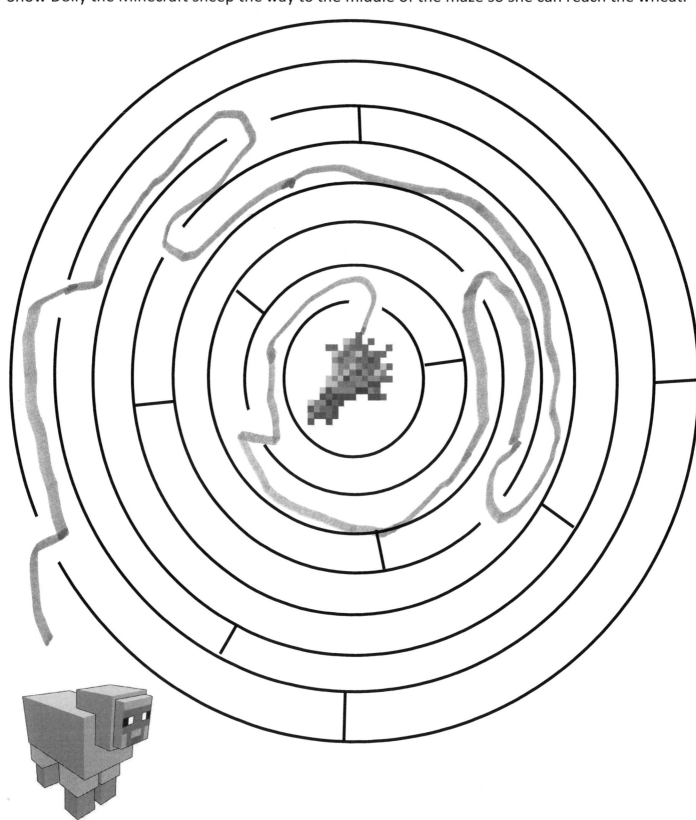

MAZES

60. WAILING GHAST

This ghast just can't stop wailing and crying! It really needs some tissues to wipe its eyes.
Show it the path through the maze to get to the box of tissues.

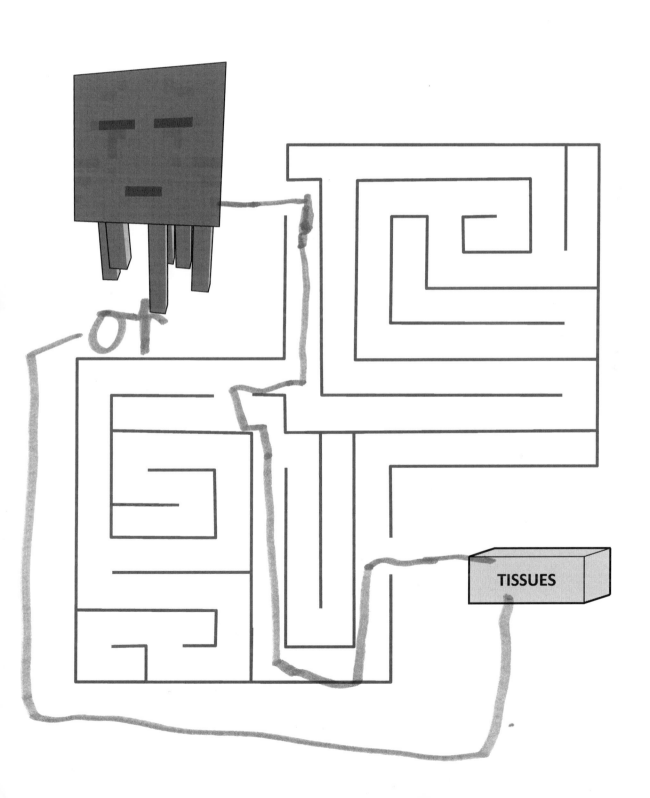

MAZES
61. SWORD SEARCH

This character wants to get to the diamond sword, but there are three entrances to the maze and he doesn't know which one to take! Find out whether he should start at entrance A, B or C and show him where to go.

MAZES
62. FIND CREEPY'S FRIEND

Creepy the creeper wants to get to his friend who is hidden at the bottom of the maze. Can you show him the way? Watch out or he will end up bumping into the ocelot.

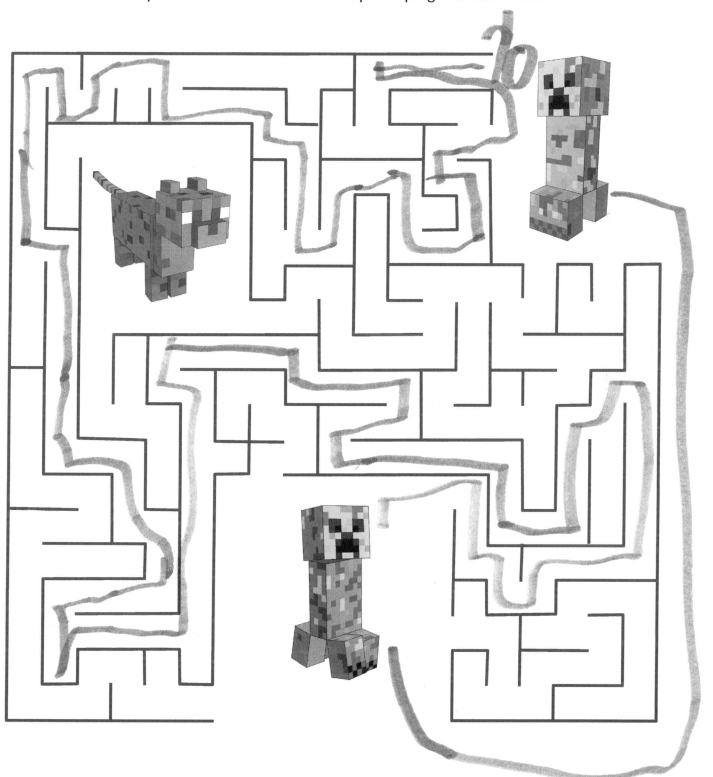

MAZES
63. HUNGER GAMES

This character is hungry. Get him through the maze so he can get to the tasty cookie. Don't send him the wrong way, or all he'll have to eat is some raw fish!

MAZES
64. NIBBLES' CARROT HUNT

Show Nibbles the Minecraft rabbit the path that takes him to the carrot in the middle.

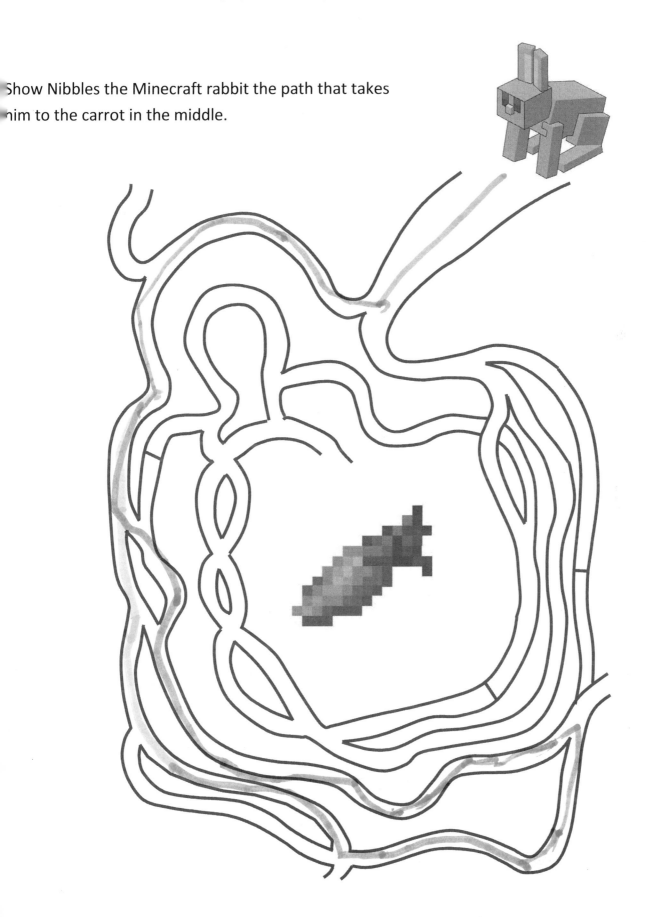

WORD PUZZLES
65. PERCY'S FOOD ANAGRAMS

Percy the Minecraft pig has set you a puzzle! He has rearranged the letters in the names of lots of things you can eat in Minecraft. Can you un-scramble them to find the answers? Percy has helped you by putting in the first letter of every answer. Good luck!

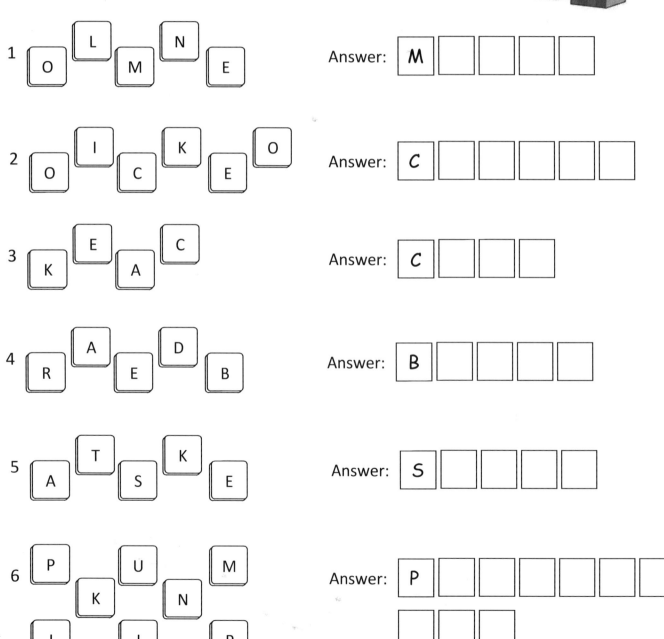

1. O L M N E

Answer: M ☐ ☐ ☐ ☐

2. O I C K E O

Answer: C ☐ ☐ ☐ ☐ ☐

3. K E A C

Answer: C ☐ ☐ ☐

4. R A E D B

Answer: B ☐ ☐ ☐ ☐

5. A T S K E

Answer: S ☐ ☐ ☐ ☐

6. P K U N M I I E P P

Answer: P ☐ ☐ ☐ ☐ ☐ ☐
☐ ☐ ☐

WORD PUZZLES
66. WOLFY'S WORD JUMBLE

Wolfy the Minecraft wolf has noticed that there are several names of blocks you can make if you use jumbled-up letters from the sentence: "MINECRAFT IS TOTALLY AWESOME, DUDE!" Complete the blank boxes to give the names of Minecraft blocks. Wolfy has helped by putting the first letter of all the blocks for you! You can use each letter as many times as you like.

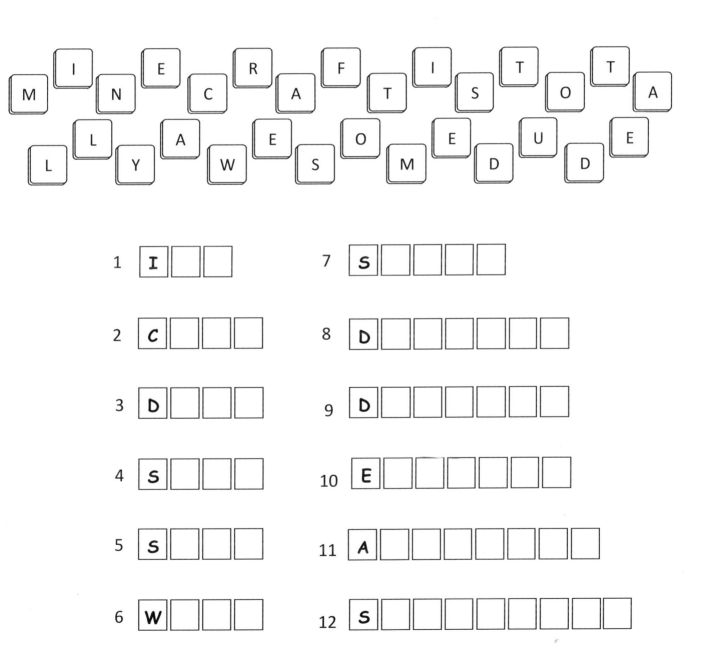

M I N E C R A F T I S T T A
L L Y A W E S O M E D U D E

1 I ☐ ☐

2 C ☐ ☐ ☐

3 D ☐ ☐ ☐

4 S ☐ ☐ ☐

5 S ☐ ☐ ☐

6 W ☐ ☐ ☐

7 S ☐ ☐ ☐ ☐

8 D ☐ ☐ ☐ ☐ ☐ ☐

9 D ☐ ☐ ☐ ☐ ☐ ☐

10 E ☐ ☐ ☐ ☐ ☐

11 A ☐ ☐ ☐ ☐ ☐ ☐ ☐

12 S ☐ ☐ ☐ ☐ ☐ ☐ ☐

WORD PUZZLES

67. FINISH THE SENTENCE

Fill in the boxes with the names of the Minecraft items shown in the pictures. Some of the boxes are shaded grey and if you have spelled the items correctly you can complete the puzzle! You will see there is an unfinished sentence at the bottom of the page. You need to copy the letters in the boxes shaded grey into the grey boxes at the bottom. Then the sentence will be complete.

Complete the sentence: ALEX LIKES

68. FINISH THE SENTENCE

Fill in the boxes with the names of the items shown. Copy the letters in the grey boxes into the boxes at the bottom to complete the sentence.

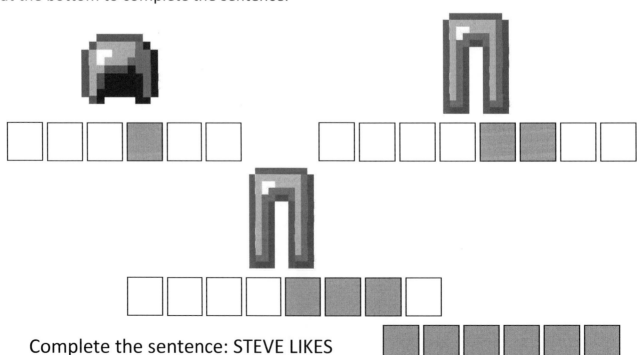

Complete the sentence: STEVE LIKES

WORD PUZZLES

69. DE-CODE THE SENTENCE

Fill in the boxes with the names of the items in the pictures. Some of the boxes are shaded grey. Copy the letters in the boxes shaded grey into the boxes at the bottom to reveal a sentence about Minecraft.

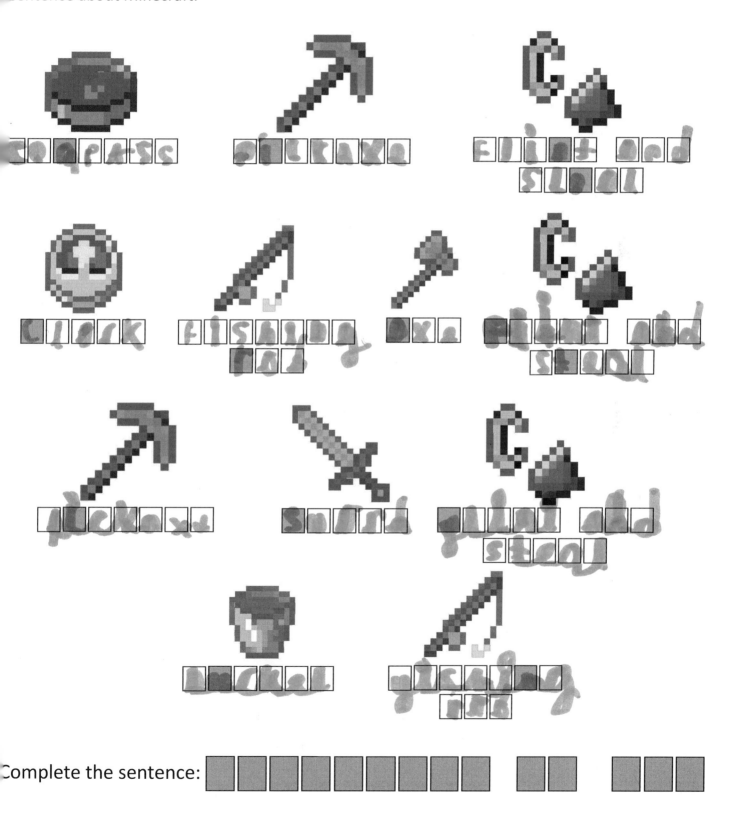

Complete the sentence:

WORD PUZZLES
70. OLLIE'S MOB ANAGRAMS

Ollie the Minecraft ocelot has messed up the letters in the names of Minecraft mobs! Can you fill the correct mob names into the blank spaces in the boxes? Ollie has filled in the first letters of all the answers to give you a head start.

1. E B M I Z O   Answer: Z O M B I E

2. E R C P E R E   Answer: c r e e p e r

3. S G H T A   Answer: G h a s t

4. H T I C W   Answer: W i t c h

5. M I S E L   Answer: s l i m e

6. L K T S E N E O   Answer: s k e l e t o n

WORD PUZZLES

71. SID'S WEAPON MIX-UP

Sid the Minecraft skeleton has mixed up the names of some weapons and tools. Can you un-jumble them and write them in the spaces? Sid has filled in the first letters to help you.

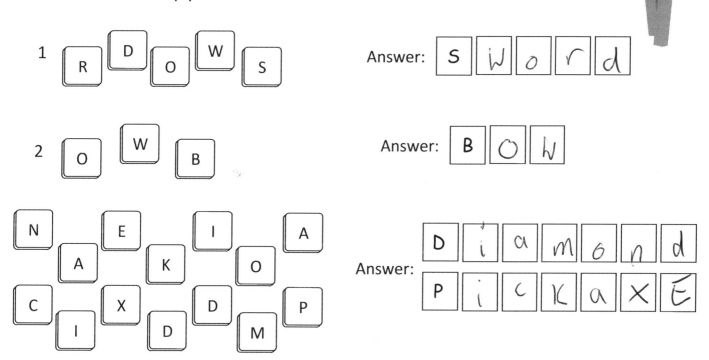

1. R D O W S — Answer: S W o r d

2. O W B — Answer: B O W

N E I A / A K O / C X D P / I D M — Answer: D i a m o n d / P i c k a x e

72. FINISH THE SENTENCE

Fill in the boxes with the names of the items in the pictures. Some of the boxes are shaded grey and if you have spelled the items correctly you can complete the puzzle! You will see there is an unfinished sentence at the bottom of the page. You need to copy the letters in the boxes shaded grey into the grey boxes at the bottom. Then the sentence will be complete.

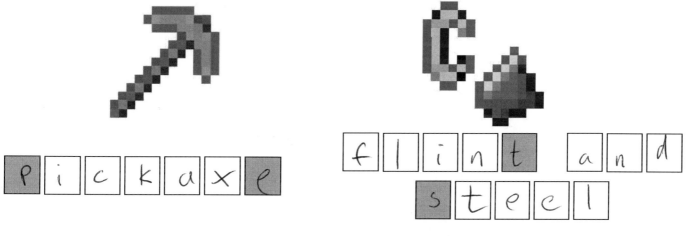

p i c k a x e

f l i n t and
s t e e l

Complete the sentence: STEVE LOVES HIS  P E t s

WORD PUZZLES
73. DOLLY'S BLOCK ANAGRAMS

Dolly the Minecraft sheep has mixed up the letters in the names of Minecraft blocks! Can you fill the correct block names into the blank spaces? Dolly has filled in the first letters of all the answers to start you off.

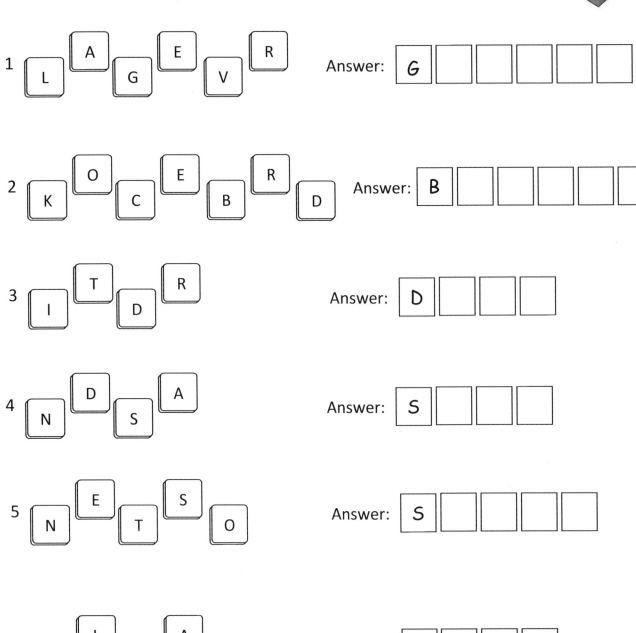

1   L A G E V R   Answer: G □ □ □ □ □

2   K O C E B R D   Answer: B □ □ □ □ □ □

3   I T D R   Answer: D □ □ □

4   N D S A   Answer: S □ □ □

5   N E T S O   Answer: S □ □ □ □

6   O L C A   Answer: C □ □ □

WORD PUZZLES: PERCY'S POEMS

Percy the Minecraft pig has written some poems, but there are some missing words! Work out the answers by thinking of words that rhyme with the words at the ends of the previous lines written in **bold**. If you choose the right words, not only will Percy's poems rhyme, they will make sense too! Good luck!

74. PERCY'S PAL POEM

My pal Steve loves his mining; to find diamond ore was his **goal**.

But rather than anything precious, all that he found was some ⬜⬜⬜⬜ !

He wanted some really good weapons, so he could feel brave as a **lion**.

But instead of finding diamonds, all that he got was some ⬜⬜⬜⬜ .

He wanted to trade with a villager, but his mining trip sure made him **moan**.

Because rather than finding emeralds, all he got was some ⬜⬜⬜⬜⬜ !

75. PERCY'S PICKAXE POEM

My friend Alex was crafting. She wanted to make something **good**.

She wanted to make a pickaxe, but she didn't have any W o o d .

She chopped down a tree to get wood then, after giving her pet wolf a **bone**.

But she didn't have any diamonds, so she made her pickaxe from S t o n e .

One day she made another, when the first one was getting quite **old**.

She still didn't have any diamonds, so she made the new one from g o l d .

WORD PUZZLES

76. NIBBLES' PLANT ANAGRAMS

Nibbles the Minecraft rabbit has mixed up the letters in the names of Minecraft plants! Can you fill the answers in the blank spaces? Nibbles has filled in the first letters of all of the jumbled-up words to help you.

1 O R W E F L

Answer: F ☐ ☐ ☐ ☐ ☐

2 O T R A R C

Answer: C ☐ ☐ ☐ ☐ ☐

3 T E R E B O T O

Answer: B ☐ ☐ ☐ ☐ ☐ ☐

4 P A N S I G L

Answer: S ☐ ☐ ☐ ☐ ☐ ☐

5 U S A C C T

Answer: C ☐ ☐ ☐ ☐ ☐

6 A T O O T P

Answer: P ☐ ☐ ☐ ☐ ☐

WORD PUZZLES

77. ANIMAL ANAGRAMS

Here are the names of Minecraft animals, but they are all mixed up! Unscramble them to find the correct animal names, and write them in the boxes.

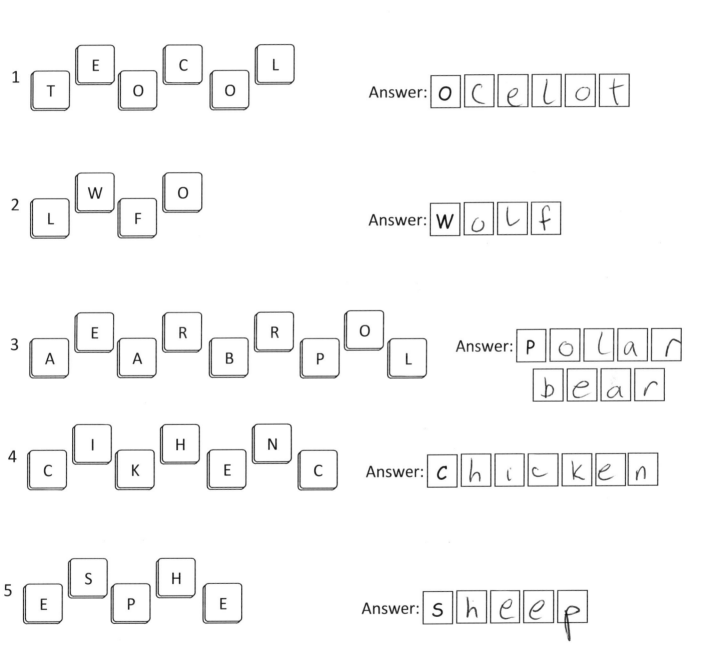

1. T E O C O L   Answer: O C e L o t

2. L W F O   Answer: W o L f

3. A E A R B R P O L   Answer: P o L a r / b e a r

4. C I K H E N C   Answer: c h i c k e n

5. E S P H E   Answer: s h e e p

6. A B T   Answer: B A T

WORD PUZZLES
78. CREEPY'S POTION ANAGRAMS

Creepy the Minecraft creeper has mixed up the letters in the names of Minecraft potions! Can you fill the correct, unscrambled words into the blank spaces? Creepy has filled in the first letters of all the answers.

1 D U M A E N
   D M N N

   Answer: M ☐ ☐ ☐ ☐ ☐

2 W D A A K
   W A R W

   Answer: A ☐ ☐ ☐ ☐ ☐

3 E S A E N S
   E A W K

   Answer: W ☐ ☐ ☐ ☐ ☐ ☐

4 I G A E
   I N H L

   Answer: H ☐ ☐ ☐ ☐ ☐

5 E S N H T
   E R T G

   Answer: S ☐ ☐ ☐ ☐ ☐ ☐

6 N I A L
   N P G E

   Answer: L ☐ ☐ ☐ ☐ ☐

WORD PUZZLES

79. FIND THE BLOCK

Write down the names of the mobs in the pictures. Then copy the letters you have put in the grey boxes into the spaces below. Rearrange these letters to find the name of a block.

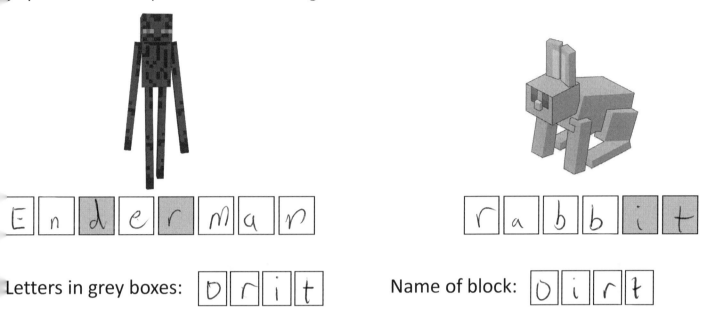

E n **d** **e** r **m** a **n**

r a **b** b **i** **t**

Letters in grey boxes: D r i t

Name of block: D i r t

80. FINISH THE SENTENCE

Fill in the boxes with the names of the items in the pictures. Copy the letters in the boxes shaded grey into the boxes at the bottom, to complete the unfinished sentence at the bottom. Can you work out what it says?

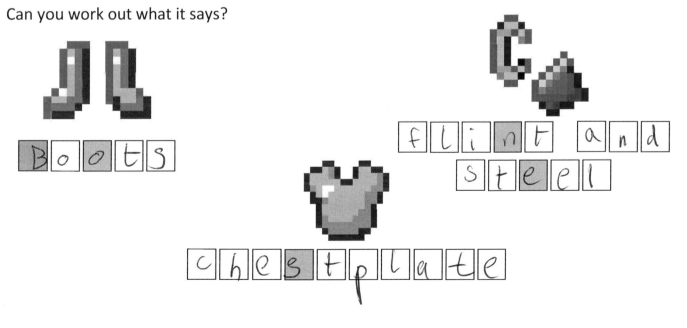

B o o t **s**

f l i **n** t a **n** d s t **e** e l

c h e **s** t p l a t e

Complete the sentence: WOLVES LIKE  B o n e s

WORD PUZZLES
81. FIND THE BLOCK

Write down the names of the mobs in the pictures. Then copy the letters you have put in the grey boxes into the spaces below. Rearrange these letters to find the name of a block.

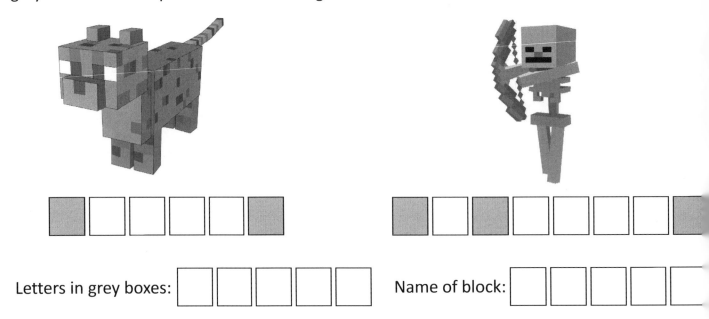

Letters in grey boxes: ☐☐☐☐☐   Name of block: ☐☐☐☐☐

82. EDDIE'S ENCHANTMENT ANAGRAMS

Eddie the Enderman has scrambled up the letters in the names of some enchantments which you can use to improve your weapons! Work out what they are and write the answers in the boxes.

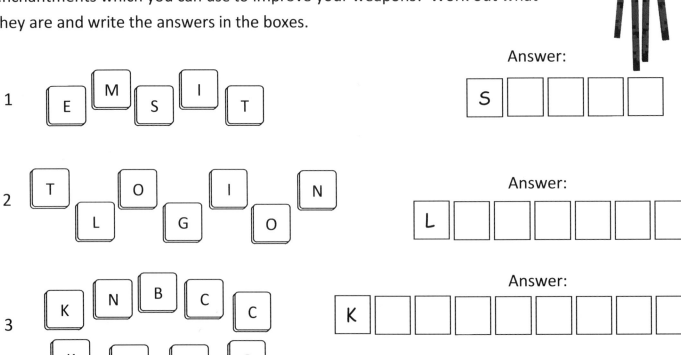

Answer:

1   E M S I T   S ☐☐☐☐

Answer:

2   T L O G I O N   L ☐☐☐☐☐

Answer:

3   K N B C C K A K O   K ☐☐☐☐☐☐☐

83. IN THE VILLAGE

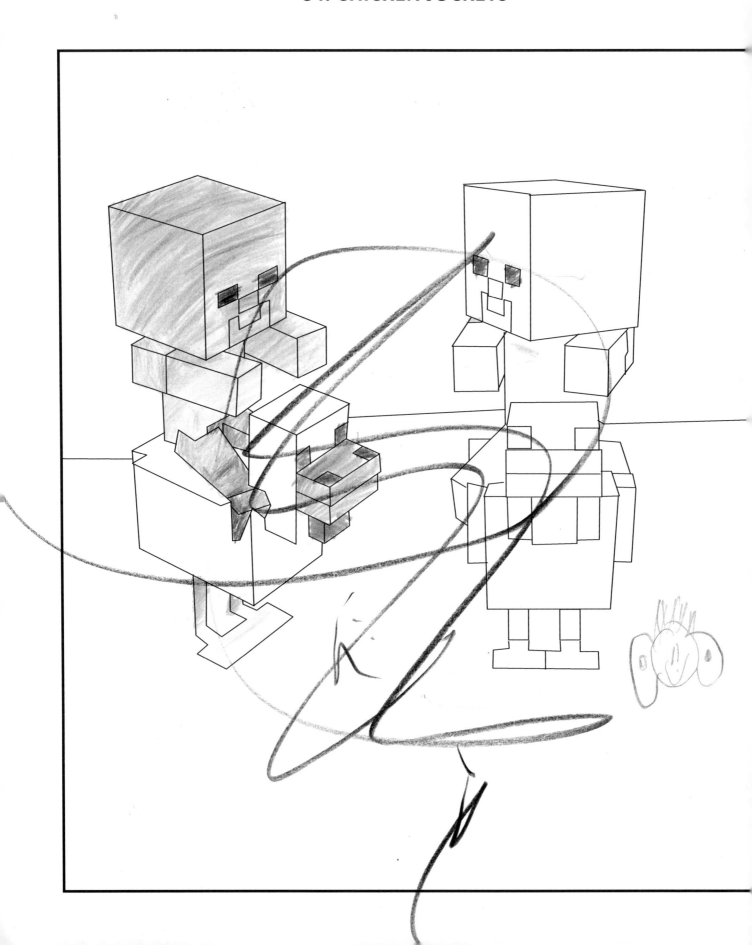

COLORING PAGES

86. MOBS ON THE MOVE

87. SKELETON HORDE

COLORING PAGES
88. WITHER ATTACK

COLORING PAGES
90. ENDER DRAGON

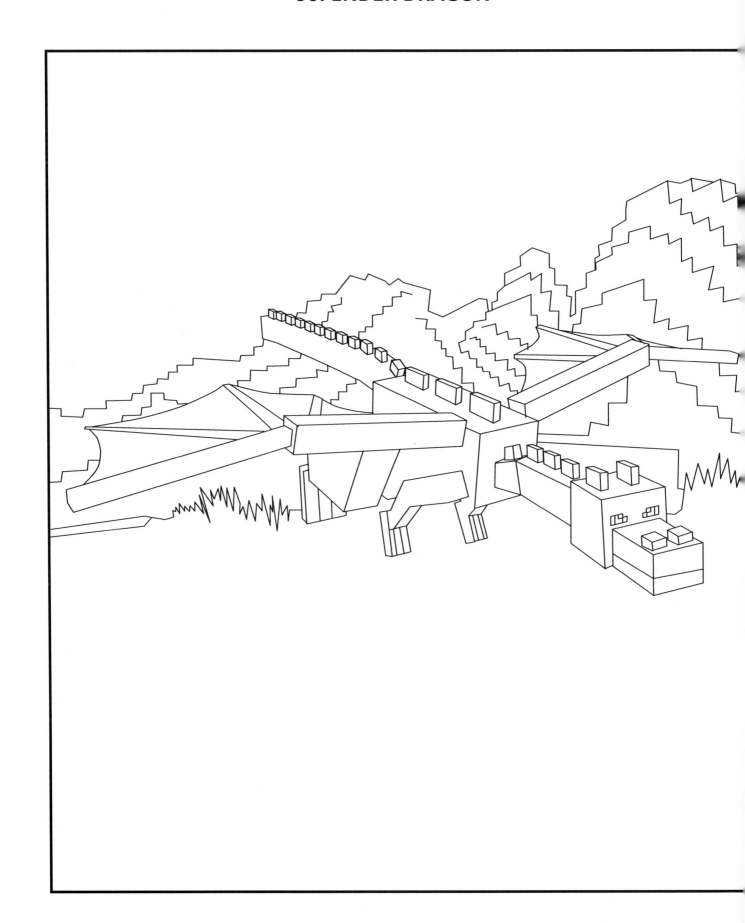

91. BLAZE

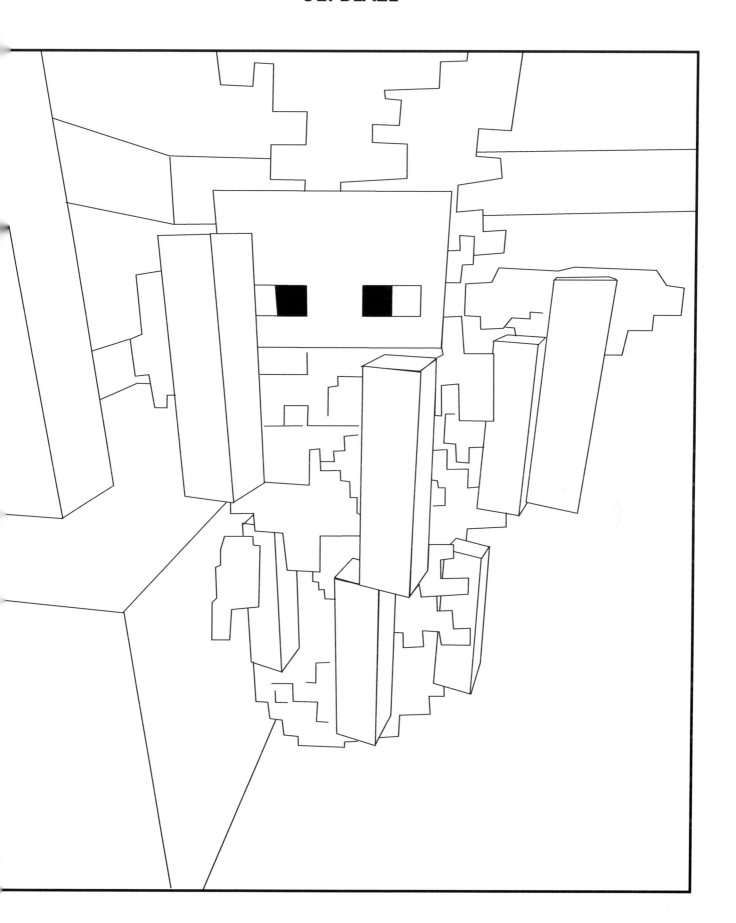

ANSWERS: PICTURE PUZZLES & WORDSEARCH

1. WHICH OCELOT?

The identical ocelot is B.

2. DOT TO DOT

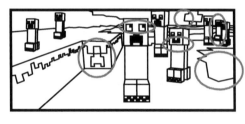

3. WHICH CREEPER?

The identical creeper is C.

4. SPOT THE DIFFERENCE

1. Big creeper's eyes have changed direction. 2. Creeper face in hillside. 3. Extra background creeper. 4. Creeper's smile is wrong. 5. Markings on ground are different. 6. Missing tree.

5. DOT TO DOT

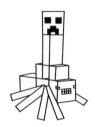

6. WHICH PIG?

The identical pig is D.

7. DOT TO DOT

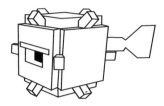

8. WHICH RABBIT?

The identical rabbit is A.

9. DOT TO DOT

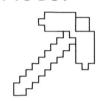

10. WHICH WOLF?

The identical wolf is A.

11. SPOT THE DIFFERENCE

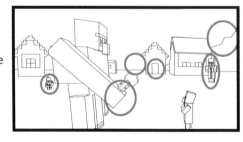

1. Golem's arm is shorter. 2. A house is missing. 3. Villager has appeared. 4. Hill in background. 5. Ocelot behind golem. 6. Door instead of window.

12. DOT TO DOT

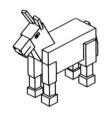

13. WHICH SKELETON?

The identical skeleton is D.

14. DOT TO DOT

15. WHICH ENDERMAN?

The identical Enderman is B.

16. DOT TO DOT

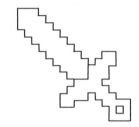

17. BOSS MOBS WORDSEARCH

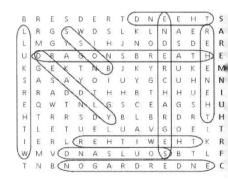

18. CREEPER WORDSEARCH

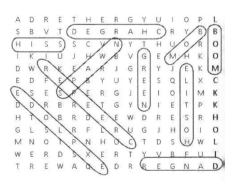

ANSWERS: WORDSEARCH

19. PIG WORDSEARCH

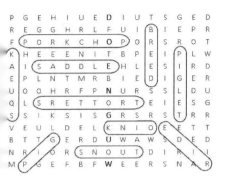

23. NEUTRAL MOBS WORDSEARCH

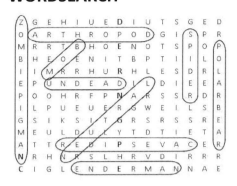

27. ENCHANTMENTS WORDSEARCH

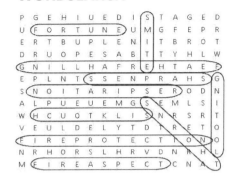

20. SKELETON WORDSEARCH

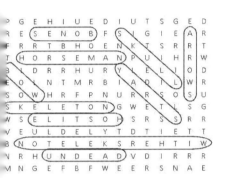

24. RABBIT WORDSEARCH

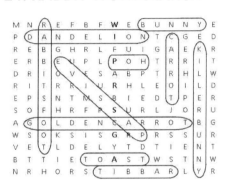

28. ILLAGERS WORDSEARCH

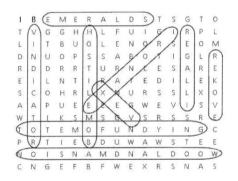

21. TAMEABLE MOBS WORDSEARCH

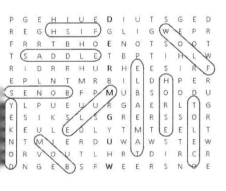

25. OCELOT WORDSEARCH

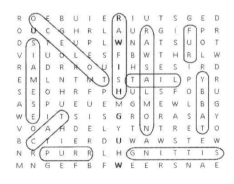

29. JUNGLE TREK WORDSEARCH

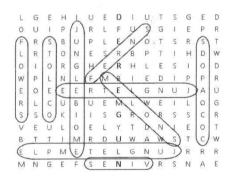

22. BIOMES WORDSEARCH

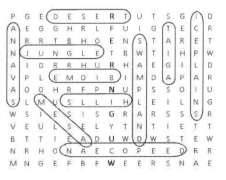

26. THE NETHER WORDSEARCH

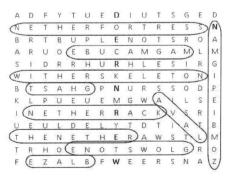

30. GOLEMS WORDSEARCH

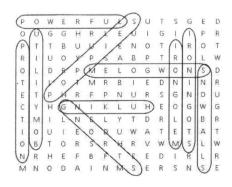

ANSWERS: WORDSEARCH & CROSSWORDS

31. THE END WORDSEARCH

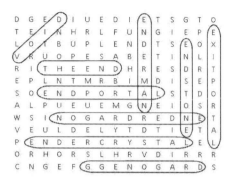

32. TOOLS WORDSEARCH

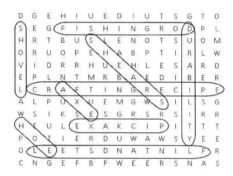

33. CROSSWORD 1

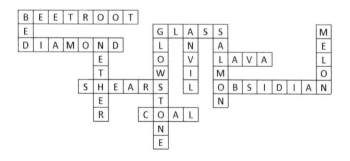

34. CROSSWORD 2

35. CROSSWORD 3

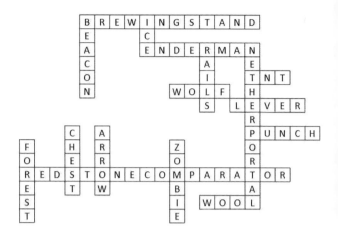

36. CROSSWORD 4

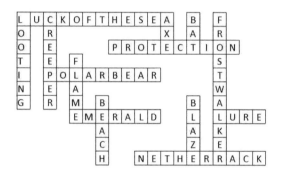

37. CROSSWORD 5

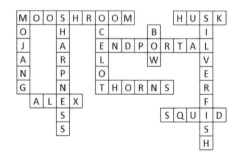

38. CROSSWORD 6

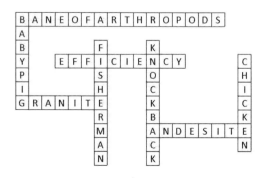

ANSWERS: CROSSWORDS

39. CROSSWORD 7

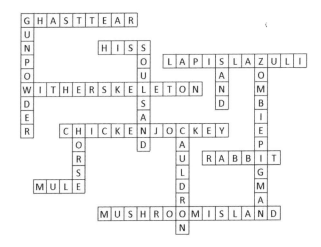

40. CROSSWORD 8

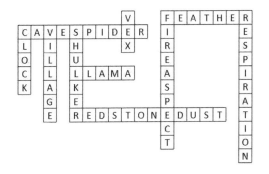

41. CROSSWORD 9

42. CROSSWORD 10

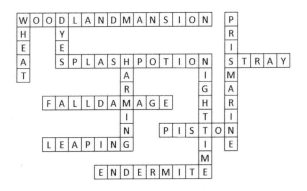

43. CROSSWORD 11

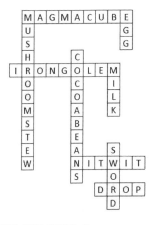

44. CROSSWORD 12

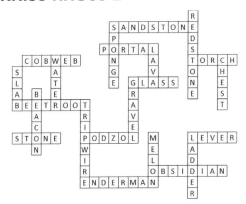

45. KRISS KROSS 1

46. KRISS KROSS 2

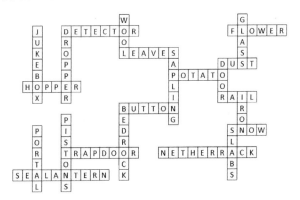

ANSWERS: KRISS KROSS

47. KRISS KROSS 3

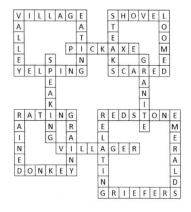

48. KRISS KROSS 4

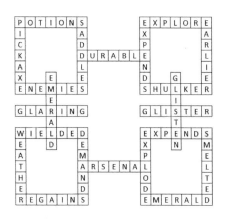

49. KRISS KROSS 5

50. KRISS KROSS 6

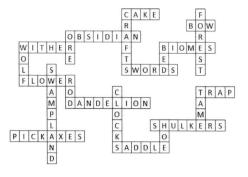

51. KRISS KROSS 7

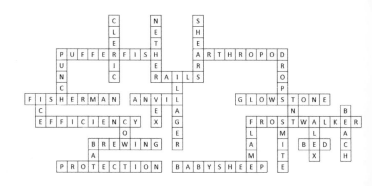

52. KRISS KROSS 8

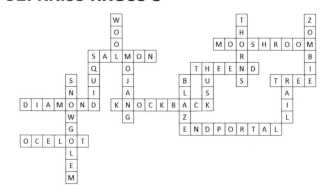

53. KRISS KROSS 9

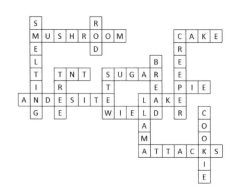

54. KRISS KROSS 10

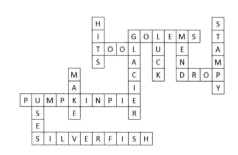

ANSWERS: KRISS KROSS & MAZES

55. KRISS KROSS 11

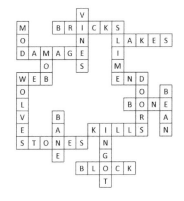

56. KRISS KROSS 12

57. HUNGRY LIKE THE WOLF

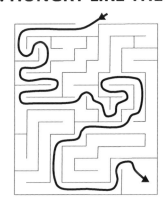

58. WEB QUEST

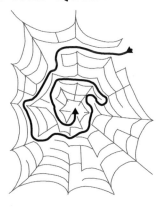

59. SHOW DOLLY THE WAY

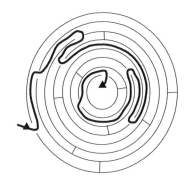

60. WAILING GHAST

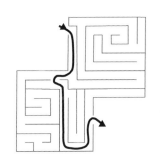

61. SWORD SEARCH

Steve needs to take entrance A to the maze.

62. FIND CREEPY'S FRIEND

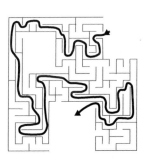

ANSWERS: MAZES & WORD PUZZLES

63. HUNGER GAMES

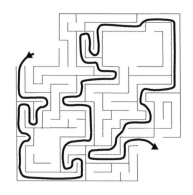

64. NIBBLES' CARROT HUNT

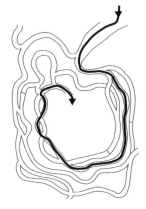

65. PERCY'S FOOD ANAGRAMS

1.	MELON	4.	BREAD
2.	COOKIE	5.	STEAK
3.	CAKE	6.	PUMPKIN PIE

66. WOLFY'S WORD JUMBLE

1.	ICE	7.	STONE
2.	COAL	8.	DIAMOND
3.	DIRT	9.	DIORITE
4.	SAND	10.	EMERALD
5.	SNOW	11.	ANDESITE
6.	WOOD	12.	SANDSTONE

67. FINISH THE SENTENCE

Items: COMPASS, CLOCK, AXE

The sentence reads: ALEX LIKES CAKE

68. FINISH THE SENTENCE

Items: HELMET, LEGGINGS, LEGGINGS

The sentence reads: STEVE LIKES MINING

69. DE-CODE THE SENTENCE

Items: COMPASS, PICKAXE, FLINT AND STEEL, CLOCK, FISHING ROD, AXE, FLINT AND STEEL, PICKAXE, SWORD, FLINT AND STEEL, BUCKET, FISHING ROD

The sentence reads: MINECRAFT IS FUN

70. OLLIE'S MOB ANAGRAMS

1.	ZOMBIE	4.	WITCH
2.	CREEPER	5.	SLIME
3.	GHAST	6.	SKELETON

71. SID'S WEAPON MIX-UP

1.	SWORD	3.	DIAMOND PICKAXE
2.	BOW		

72. FINISH THE SENTENCE

Items: PICKAXE, FLINT AND STEEL

The sentence reads: STEVE LOVES HIS PETS

ANSWERS: WORD PUZZLES

73. DOLLY'S BLOCK ANAGRAMS

1. GRAVEL
2. BEDROCK
3. DIRT
4. SAND
5. STONE
6. COAL

74. PERCY'S PAL POEM

Missing words: COAL, IRON, STONE

75. PERCY'S PICKAXE POEM

Missing words: WOOD, STONE, GOLD

76. NIBBLES' PLANT ANAGRAMS

1. FLOWER
2. CARROT
3. BEETROOT
4. SAPLING
5. CACTUS
6. POTATO

77. ANIMAL ANAGRAMS

1. OCELOT
2. WOLF
3. POLAR BEAR
4. CHICKEN
5. SHEEP
6. BAT

78. CREEPY'S POTION ANAGRAMS

1. MUNDANE
2. AWKWARD
3. WEAKNESS
4. HEALING
5. STRENGTH
6. LEAPING

79. FIND THE BLOCK

Mobs: ENDERMAN, RABBIT

Name of block: DIRT

80. FINISH THE SENTENCE

Items: BOOTS, FLINT AND STEEL, CHESTPLATE

The sentence reads: WOLVES LIKE BONES

81. FIND THE BLOCK

Mobs: OCELOT, SKELETON

Name of block: STONE

82. EDDIE'S ENCHANTMENT ANAGRAMS

1. SMITE
2. LOOTING
3. KNOCKBACK

Printed in Great
Britain
by Amazon